Poems from
the Winter House

Daniel Smith

Poems from the Winter House

Daniel Smith

Water's Edge Press

Printed in the United States of America

Water's Edge Press LLC
Tucson, AZ
watersedgepress.com

ISBN: 978-1-952526-13-8

Library of Congress Control Number: 2023934629

Credits:
Jim Harrison, excerpt from "Returning to Earth" from the
Essential Poems. Copyright © 1977 by Jim Harrison. Reprinted
with the permission of The Permissions Company, LLC on
behalf of Copper Canyon Press, coppercanyonpress.org.

Photo of Smith home from family archives. Cover photo by the
author. Artistic design by Ryan Smith, MD and Water's Edge Press.
Author photo by Cheryl Smith. Interior image licensed by iStock.

A WATER'S EDGE PRESS FIRST EDITION

This book is for Cheryl,
who makes the Winter House a home,
and for our grandchildren,
who bring in the light.

In the Absence of a Farm

To Words

The Lies I Tell Myself

"We are each
the only world
we are going to get."

Jim Harrison
Returning To Earth

The Winter House, Wisconsin, 2022

These logs of white pine felled in the north country, trucked south
to Wisconsin, hoisted in place, fitted seamless with notched corners,
gaps carefully caulked, so that in years to come they warmly hold
two lives lived in the glow of the fire on winter evenings
as the hollow fills with snow.

Now we know it is possible to love more than one place.

Coming here, we carried with us all that came before, all we had
become. Come close, sit with me in the window of the Winter House.
A good day is drawing down. The cold, white stars are above us
and the long winter night lies ahead.

In the Absence of a Farm

In the Absence of a Farm

Weather is just weather, wet or dry,
hot or cold, something controlled
by the turn of a thermostat.

Walks are over public land, around
Devil's Lake or down the trail
bordering Black Earth Creek.

Come chore time, I fill bird feeders,
rake leaves, buzz the weed whipper
around the flower bed out front.

For the first time in my life, I've not
a single machine in need of repair, not
one animal down in the sick pen.

Empty silos, barren barns, fields
in need of the cultivator will keep
someone else awake all night.

Let it rain – or not. In the absence of a farm
I live a life of diminished concern,
my farmer tan slowly fading away.

Time

is a gift
I've heard it said

time
and time again

now it is time
I count on

as time goes by
one day at a time

flying
beneath timeless stars

celestial trackers
of all time

lend me their light
grant me their galaxy

for I have aways
to go

over hills
across valleys

one step at a time

Memory of My Mother, Burning Trash

From the farmhouse, she crossed
the yard, head down,
bound for the burn barrel.

She carried odds and ends,
the week's newspapers,
old food wrappers.

From afar, I watched her
strike the match.
I saw smoke rise.

She stood staring
far off toward something
only she could see.

I should have gone to her
but what does a child know
about the weight of a life?

I stayed my distance, frightened
of the fire,
well clear of the smoke.

Things Picked Up Along the Way

The brass buckles of a bridle
found in the drawer of a workbench
on a farm in Illinois.

A small, round stone
some sort of dark gray quartz
pocketed from a campsite in the Dakotas.

A billfold lost years ago
then found empty behind books
the day we moved north to Wisconsin.

A torn photo of you at eighteen
lovely blonde hair to your waist
our first visit to my brother in Missouri.

A dog-eared copy, yellow with age
of *Grass Beyond the Mountains*
my favorite book from childhood.

The single feather of a chicken hawk
picked up on a day just like today
hiking the north trail at Blue Mounds.

A handmade nativity set
made from pine and porcelain
my mother bought decades ago in Milwaukee.

The sight of my father's fingers
threading twine through a New Holland baler
out west of the dairy barn in Harlem Township.

Resolution

Enough of this standing around
like Billy Ott's dummy.

By now I should know better.

Tomorrow I'll get up
and get going, I swear on my life.

Just you watch and see.

Segmented Sleep

Up and about at three in the morning, water glass in hand

Finding my way in darkness, feet feeling the floorboards

Peering out from the Winter House, snow filling the hollow

Looking for deer, listening for coyotes

Checking the stove, feeding wood to last until morning

Heading back down the hall, shivering in the chill

Slipping under the covers, moving close to steal your warmth

Satisfied all is well, sighing, sliding softly toward sleep

Buyer's Remorse

We held a mortgage
so heavy
two generations signed.

My mother wondered
if we'd live long enough
to burn it.

So much to pay off
milking cows
twice a day, every day.

Better hope we find oil
under the farm.

Better pick winning numbers
for Powerball.

The Beam in the Barn

Long ago, long
before I moved here, a man
hanged himself from a beam
in the barn.

Some days, in a mood,
I go and look up, imagining
the slow, deliberate climb
and exquisite fall.

When they cut him down
they cut the beam down, too,
creating a gap in the gables,
forever marking the spot.

Now, years later, I enter
the dark loft, fingers entwined
like rope, eyeing the beams,
gauging the drop.

My Hands, In Winter

The day dies slow as a gut-shot deer.

At chore time, I go out, seeking chores.

Something to fix, feed, bed down for the night.

I pull off my heavy gloves, give my hands to the cold.

When I go in, I warm them over the fire.

I rub them red and raw.

I make believe they've been busy, working.

Doing something worth doing.

After the Horse Died

Now I have time
to linger.

I stay in the barn,
tending a few chores.

I store away the bridle,
curry comb and brush.

I saddle soap
the saddle and set it aside.

I toss out a half pail of oats
mice managed to find.

The last of the hay
will do for garden mulch.

When the wind rattles
the pasture gate,

I look out to see
what is no longer there.

Two Hearts

West of River Road
just north of the river
in a stand of burr oak
and jack pine
he was found
beside the eight-point
buck
he tracked
then leveled
with a shot
to the heart
making it
two
that gave out
at dusk
Thanksgiving Day
when he failed
to come home
the turkey cold
gravy congealed
the family
getting up
heading out
beginning the search
fearing the worst

Poem

To awake is to have survived
the night.

Now – the day awaits –
   an ice-covered road
      through bad country.

Keep two hands on the wheel.
Keep a foot on the brakes.

There are people
who love you
waiting in the distance.

Go on now.

Give it some gas.

Burn the cold white miles
one-by-one
out from the rearview mirror.

Barnfire

The night our barn burned my mother
led me
to the edge of the yard.

The view was all yellow flame
and smoke
where our cows had stood.

Aunt Harriet and Uncle Frank
drove out from town
in their green Rambler.

They brought bread, bologna
and cheese –
sandwiches for the fire crew.

At the kitchen table
I watched
as they wrapped each in wax paper.

They placed them
in the brown paper bags
we used for school lunches.

Then carried them
in their arms
out across the farmyard

toward the fire,
like offerings to the altar
during Sunday morning Mass.

The Shack

Weathered wooden
sides

rusted tin roof
leaking snowmelt
and rain

floor of trampled dirt

one cane-back chair
and
one table made of an old door

to get there
you must walk

one step at a time

away from the Winter House
across the fallowed fields

into the dark woods

carefully
open the door

it hangs on a single hinge

then go in

go in

A Thought

On a morning
like this
I would give
anything
to be
that wren
at the feeder
living life
one tiny seed
at a time

Farm Country

Time was a farmer raised a family
on thirty cows and twelve sows.

Made a living
by the careful cultivation of crops
and proper use of farm implements.

Before the land grant colleges
graduated a generation of land grabbers,
every farm had a farmer.

Now the cracked roads of farm country
grow grass.

Commodities – not crops – fill the fields,
cultivated by drones, sprayed with poison.

You might ask the falling farms
and the hollow towns what happened
but there is no one left
to answer.

New Neighbors

On move-in day, our new neighbor
shows up, offering a hand.

"I'm Del. I'm eighty years old and I still sleep
in the room where I was born."

I acknowledge the hierarchy.

I tell him where we've come from, the farm
and the work we've left behind.

He wants to know
if I miss the cows and I tell him
I do.

He laughs.

"I missed mine, too.
Took me a good fifteen minutes
to get over it."

Outside the COVID Clinic, Plain, Wisconsin

One after another, the at-risk emerge
from salt splattered cars
and trucks.

They shuffle across asphalt,
confirmation of their appointment
fluttering like white flags.

They pass cohorts who come out
rubbing their arms, squinting
into the bare light of a lost winter.

Now immune, feeling invincible,
they light cigarettes, pause,
ponder the rest of the day.

Across the street a blue
Trump/Pence sign dips and drains
into a bank of melting snow.

Culver's for lunch? A man suggests.

Why not? His wife replies,
suddenly hungry with only time to kill.

Old Work

In the late afternoon, in the old shed, sunlight
falls across the workbench, catches in the vise.

There are tools here I've not used in years –
wrenches, hammers, drills, pry bars –

hauled up from a farm in Illinois
a long time ago when I was someone else.

They hang from spikes pounded into walls.
They lean on each other in dark corners.

Always within reach should something break,
give out, wear down, crack in the cold.

Like transients on the street, waiting
for someone to come along, offering work.

Questions

An owl called all night
from the woods above the Winter House.

What was he asking of this world?

Unable to sleep, pacing through old regrets
and new worries, I kept asking myself the same.

To Go Back

All my days
have grown into years
tall and tangled
as a neglected hedgerow.

If I dropped
to my hands and knees
and crawled across the ground
I'd never make it through.

Even if I did
it would be like
opening a coffin
expecting to find life.

In the Farmhouse

You prayed trouble
stay down in the barn.

The breach birth of a calf,
dead before hitting the straw.

The fresh heifer with a blank quarter,
or winter dysentery sweeping the herd.

A cracked water pipe,
or bad bearing in the milk pump.

But you knew damn well
trouble has a way of busting out,

scurrying across the dark farmyard
like a rat from the burn pile.

You hear it in the night, scratching,
making its way up the basement stairs.

You want to hide there in the darkness
but you get up and reach for your boots.

Beyond the Hayfield

Mowed swaths dry
in the sun of a Sunday morning.

There is a scent
that makes me want to be a boy again.

It is like a drug
craved only by those born to farming.

It is an addiction
to a life and work that no longer exists.

Given time, the aroma
will fade, dissipate, drift away.

The bare stubble
will begin its long task of recovery.

In this new life
I keep working to do the same.

Old Wounds

The lift and crossover swing
of the milking machine
lives on
in my fingers, wrists, shoulders.

When I walk,
postholes dug long ago
and the dead lift of hay bales
grind bone on bone down my spine.

Nights when I sleep – nights
few and far between –
I dream of too little rain,
not enough feed, too many chores.

I am what I am – an old farmer
hoarding old wounds, filling up
the aging bins of my body,
the leaning barns of my brain.

When a Farm Falls Apart

Nails loosen in the boards of the pasture fence
Below the ground, corner posts soften with rot
No one comes running with a hammer and spade
No one comes running

Short on feed, the cattle are turned out
Onto early pasture short on feed
Flies swarm around the horned heads
Of unvaccinated calves long past calfhood

It starts with round bales yanked from a fence row
Dumped into a feeder deep in manure
Next comes an Angus bull let loose on Holsteins
Then comes part-time work selling trinkets in town

Blinded by barn blindness and short on time
Hacking up a farmer's lung burned by silo gas
No one trims the box elder overgrown in the lane
No one repairs the busted-out window in the barn

Morning chores run into afternoon chores
Over lunch cross words fly across the kitchen
A letter from the bank lies unopened on the table
Like dirt in a dry July it all just up and blows away

Buying Heifers With My Father in the 70s

Gas up the '65 Dodge stock truck. Let it run – turn the heat
on high. Toss in insulated coveralls, hats, heavy flannel mittens.
Head north and pull in at Reed's for coffee, cigars, cigarettes.

Park along the road and walk in through the long line of equipment.
Heavy farm iron and rod made for choring or cropping. Hear the
auctioneer's cry and the yelp of the ring hands. Nod to neighbors, talk
of cold weather, low prices, who is buying and who's next to sell out.

Find the warmth of the stanchion barn – 60 cows – 30
down each side. All Holsteins. Good feet, legs, udders.
Flanks trimmed. Tails clean. Generations of Select Sires
breeding. Good quality milk shipped to the cheese plant in
Monroe. Low somatic and high butterfat. DHIA records on
the milk house wall prove a high rolling herd average.

Look over a half-dozen yearlings in a pen out back in the
shelter of the loafing shed. Good cover over their ribs.
Eyes clear. No coughing, hacking, or wet noses. Calfhood
vaccinated by the vets out of Lena. Dehorned. With good
feed, fit to breed in three months, milking in twelve.

Wait in line at the FFA lunch table in the machine shed.
Shredded pork on a bun with a bag of chips and coffee for two
bucks. Check to see if they've finished up selling equipment.
Yes, they're onto the feed. Heifers are next, then cows.

We're at the pen before the crew arrives. Dad lights a cigar and
acts uninterested. The auctioneer steps up onto a hay bale. He
raves on the six heifers as the ring hands turn them around
and around in the pen, hooves pounding flat the straw.

He starts the bidding high, then lower, then lower again until someone nods. Yep, yells the ring hand. And we're off, each bid $25 over the last. I stare straight ahead. Dad draws on his cigar. Keeps his hat low over his eyes. He bids with the slightest nod of his head. The low bidders drop out. It is Dad and a big, red-faced dairyman across the way in a Kent Feeds cap. Dad nods at $750 and the Kent Feeds guy shakes his head and walks away. We've got ourselves six heifers.

It's tight but they fit into the stock truck. Tight is good, Dad says. It will keep them from bouncing around. He drives slow under the load, lights a cigarette, talks about the farms we pass – who lived there once and who farms it now. The truck smells like warm manure, wet boots, and the smoke of an unfiltered Camel.

By dark we've got them penned up in the heifer shed. Let's keep them separate tonight, Dad says. We'll let them get settled. Toss in two bales of hay and check the water. I'll start chores. They look like good ones. There will be a hole in the checkbook for a while but they're worth it. He leaves for the milk house. I think how it's been a good day. A good day for buying heifers with my father.

The View from the Winter House Window

One silver coyote
on a dead run
across the open field
at high noon

———

The frantic feeding
of wrens, cardinals, sparrows
blown up by the arrival
of a solitary blue jay

———

Six-inch snowfall
not a thing moving
but the flashing lights
of the township plow

———

Unable to sleep
after late news of trouble
a tired old man
looks in through the pane

———

The rural route mailman
swerves his rusted Chrysler
close to the mailbox
shoves in the daily junk

———

Black coffee in hand
suddenly startled
by the thought
of my mother's death bed

Hoar frost on the trees
icy roads and north wind
if I was a cook
I'd make biscuits and gravy

Winter House windows
are all deep-set glass
good for looking out
wondering what's out there

Life is now as I feared
one man alone in a window
watching the day end
wishing to God you were here

That broken barn window
I meant to fix last summer
comes in handy
for pigeons coming home

The whole day ahead
I look out wondering
who'll I'll hear from
what might go wrong

———◆———

Evening and now I see
a light left on in the barn
I'll pull on my boots
stomp over and flip a switch

———◆———

All those white stars
in a black winter sky
each one has a view
worth dying for

———◆———

At four in the morning
staring out a dark window
after all these years
still feeling it is time to milk

The Day We Sold the Cows

I awoke to rain
and walked out
to milk
one last time.

We'd been at it
thirty years.

Twice a day,
everyday.

Name me one thing
that lasts forever.

After the loading,
the gates stayed open
like unstitched wounds.

I walked up
and found you on the porch.

You asked if it was over.

We held each other,
looking out past the empty barn
as if somehow, we might see
what was coming.

To Words

To Words

The first words to my ears
came low across the prairie
like rocks rolled
over virgin ground.

Uttered by German and Irish farmers,
filed to a point, pointing
to bad weather and broken machinery
and horses that could no longer pull.

Filled with dead furrows, headlands,
summer fallow and busted bearings.
With hoar frost, open heifers,
twisted stomachs and stillborn calves.

At the workbench, in the field
or out back of the barn,
I learned swear words
that never made it to the house.

There, men grew silent. Heads down,
they shoveled food like coal into a furnace,
red forearms placed before their plates,
never looking up, lost for words.

To Memory

A two-track farm lane
through land that you love

On a warm morning
in late June and you a child

There are meadowlarks
perched upon cedar fence posts

There are redwing blackbirds
and ringtail pheasants

The small herd of cows
that pay the bills are in deep grass

Everyone you love
is alive and close to home

Soon you will sit with them
over sandwiches and white milk

The plastic future is unknown
and you are unaware of passage

You pull off your shirt
to walk in the safe sunlight

Little puffs of clean soil
lift from beneath your footsteps

To a Dream

My father was alive and young and his arms
were strong, burned by the sun the way I remember.

There were still white board fences
around the farmyard and the barn was straight and true.

The twin oaks that fell in an August storm in '65
shaded the yard and two big willows stood by the pond.

Someone, I don't know who, was curing meat
in the brick smokehouse. I could almost smell the smoke.

A door opened and my mother came out into the yard,
her black hair hung straight and long, the color of night.

When I awoke, I found it hard to breathe,
like I had been running a long, long way.

I lay there not moving, sorting through the images,
putting them into an order I could recognize.

To Marriage

This world is filled with miracles
walking shoulder to shoulder.

In step, seeing the same shapes,
speaking similar words, in unison.

Laughing at something yet to appear.
Leaving unspoken, old slights, old barbs.

Then, turning toward home,
turning together, walking together

through the shared day,
toward the falling dark.

To What We Wore

There was that long hippie skirt
you bought at *Sunshine Daydream* on State Street.

I wore my *New Riders of the Purple Sage* t-shirt.

Cowboy boots were a poor choice
for Wisconsin winters
but I was making a point.

Pachouli.

Blonde hair way past your shoulders.
Brown to mine.

My dad's DeKalb Seed Corn jacket,
emblazed with a flying ear of corn.

Turquoise earrings
and the gold necklace you still wear.

My brass belt buckle.
The pearl snaps of my western shirt.

The white crocheted shawl
I gave you our first Christmas.

I recall how it covered your shoulders,
how it kept you warm that winter
a half-century ago.

To a Photo of My Grandfather

I've done the math. It has been
three-quarters of a century.

I was ten years from existing.
By the time I arrived, you were gone.

How tall you stood, confident, proud,
in a suit with overcoat, galoshes, fedora.

It was winter. You were outside
in the cold near big piles of snow.

You must have been on a farm that day,
a wooden corncrib stands in the background.

To know more – the way you spoke
or things you read or enjoyed,

I would have to ask my father
but he is gone now, too.

I look, and look again, hoping to see
something of myself

but too much time has passed, the black
and white image too faded to claim.

To a Barn Barely Standing

The wind enters, swirls, departs
like breath through the lungs
of an old man dying.

The stars and moon drain down
though the splintered shingles.

Now the sun strikes what was dark.
The rain soaks what was dry.

Years since the haymakers took leave.
Since cows shook the steel stanchions.

So – what will it be –
      gust of wind, lightning, snow load
      upon your rotting rafters?

It is all the same –
      one more chore
      that needs to be done.

And who knows chores
      better than you?

To This Country Life

Each day is built of similar stock.

We watch daylight reveal
the edges of the fields.

We drink coffee.
We read the news.

Over breakfast – something light –
an egg or sliced fruit –
you ask what I might like for lunch.

Then you tell me what we'll be having
and I applaud.

You reserve the afternoon for reading.
You *absolutely love* your book.

But first, a hike, and later,
another, over trails hiked so many times
the land feels like our own.

An old friend writes to suggest a cruise
or a weekend in the city.

We defer. We can't possibly.

We are far too busy
doing what it is we do all day.

To the Storm

I am sorry I missed you.
A sound sleeper, I was unaware.

You left your calling card
with the big white pine that stood
a half century
west of the cabin.

I would have preferred you had not
but I know
you have a way with wind and rain.

Just as I do, with chainsaw and tractor,
trimming and quartering
all the broken branches

beneath
 the wide expanse of open sky
you created.

To Whistling

My son is an early riser.

When I stay with him in old St. Paul,
he is up and at it
an hour before sunrise.

He wakes me with the rattle
of pots and pans, the clatter of plates.

When I smell coffee, I head down.

From the hallway, I hear him whistling.

I pause but cannot place the tune.

Still, it is a beautiful thing
for a father to hear
before NPR comes with the news,
before my phone fills with texts.

And suddenly, I find myself
looking ahead, believing somehow,
we will all be okay.

To the Woodpecker

You might think to leave the cabin alone.

After all, there's forty acres of woods –
all those dead trees
just a stone's throw away.

And I've hung suet in wire baskets
all around the yard.

You really can't miss them.

But still you do.

It is a good thing I have no neighbors.

They'd call the cops
over my swearing and threatening.

But you just peer down at me
from the new hole
you are boring in the eaves –

jabbing your pointed beak
and ruffling your feathers –

as you keep on doing
exactly
what woodpeckers do.

To Melancholy

In the midst of too much
carrying on
too many loud voices
calling from a train platform
announcing arrivals
and departures
too many people
in a hurry
to get somewhere
to do nothing
I slip away
unnoticed
shuffling my feet
hoping no one
calls my name
pulls me back
into the present
forcing me to do
something
I would rather not
leave me in the past
it fits
like an old coat
well-worn
always warm
comfortable
lined with
everything I've
picked up
brushed off
stuffed
into my pockets
all along the way

To the Rain

Rise up
out of afternoon heat

Then fall
give the haymakers a break

Seep down
beneath the knee-high corn

Lightly scatter
pollen across the flower bed

Wash clean
the dusty car parked in the yard

Give way
to clearing and then evening

Come back
when the corn leaves curl

To an Act of Arson

Enough time has passed, enough distance built, that we might now examine the evidence, imagine the unimaginable, contemplate the criminality of what occurred in a single night by the hand of one man.

A family man. A man of the land. At home on the land, in the work of farming. At home in the big clapboard house with his wife and five young children. A pastoral existence to those passing by, to those unaware of the smoldering kindling stacked beneath.

That night, normal by all indications – supper with friends in the café of a small, Midwestern town. A few beers. Talk of farming, families, and the holidays ahead. Tired, wanting rest, he leaves the party and drives his truck back to the farm and his sleeping children.

From the farm tank (the one for fueling implements of husbandry) he fills red jerry cans of diesel fuel and enters the family home, fumes following his footfalls up and down the papered hallways, the carpeted stairwell, past the family photos and along the painted baseboards.

Finished, worn out, done with his work, he lights a copy of the *Stephenson County Farmer* and tosses the flaming torch down the stairs. He goes into the room he shared twenty years with his wife. He lies down on their marriage bed and waits.

In the morning, the volunteer firemen of the Rock City Fire District – men with day jobs in insurance, plumbing, construction, men with families of their own – refused to retrieve the six blackened bodies. They went home. Some cried. Some stared hours at the wall, unable to unsee the horror.

The state sent a team out from Chicago where they know
how to deal with such things, how to clean everything up
and bury the debris of a life. There was a short notice and
six obits in the local paper. A bulldozer erased the farmstead
and the land sold to someone from out-of-state.

A year or more passed, then, with little acknowledgment, the
county corner ruled murder/suicide by an act of arson. Just a box
checked on a form filed in a courthouse drawer. Concise. Factual.
No reason or explanation stated. An act devoid of comprehension.

There are things we cannot talk about until the years disguise the
facts, until grass hides the graves, until faces and names blur and fade.
Then, we realize how little we see when we look into a man's eyes.
Behind them may well be a door we best pray stays shut and bolted.

To Evening

Let snow begin in late afternoon.
You are home
and there is no place you need to go.

The wood box holds split elm.
The watched pot boils.
The oven warms.

Set the table for two.
Light candles. Cue Lord Huron.
Decant a Syrah.

You know it will not always be this way.

Gather evening.

Hold it like that one field
of a thousand fields that summer
cutting wheat out west.

It was in southern Kansas, south
of the co-op grain bins.

The wheat wavered in the late light.
Shadows drained in from the edges.

There were a few old cottonwoods
and beyond them a small creek moved crossways
like the barrel of a gun.

You wanted it all to stay forever the same.

But then you started the combine.

You lowered the sickle bar.

You turned in
and began the task
of cutting it all to chaff.

To My Dog

Don't look at me
that way.

Those sad eyes
burning with *your* needs.

Can't you see I'm busy here,
making a living?

Well, okay.
But just to the road and back.

I'm on the clock
and someone around here
has to pay the bills.

To Things Unsaid

Worry less words said
than unsaid.

All the missed chances
for clarity and wisdom.

Later, lying awake in the dark
or walking through the village
or drinking in a bar,

you think of exactly
what you should have said

had cat not got your tongue.

To Downsizing

Burn and purge, sort
through things not held in years,
toss what is trash.

Polish the tarnished heirlooms,
candlesticks, platters, tea sets.
Wrap them in felt

and pass them on,
pass them down,
grant them new lives.

Donate what others might use.
Remember, one man's junk
is another's treasure.

Admire the quiet beauty
of a clean closet,
of a bare basement.

Save a warm sweater, cap,
rain jacket and boots
for when the weather turns.

Sweep the floorboards clean.
Run an oiled rag along the woodwork.
Wipe down the wainscoting.

Leave everything as it was.
Now, when the bell sounds,
you'll be like Han Shan,

light afoot, unencumbered, free,
out the door, empty pockets
flapping in the breeze.

To Surviving Cold Winters

Top off the wood pile. Fill the coal bin. Hoard kindling.

Wrap the screened porch in ten-gauge plastic held by furring strips.

Do the same with the windows.

Stack straw bales along the north and west
foundation of the farmhouse.

Close off unused rooms. Live close to the heart of the house.

Leave a faucet drip a stream the size of pencil lead.

Pile snow over the well pit.

Imitate the hired man with his bottle of Rock & Rye
hid in the rafters of the barn – antifreeze for the blood.

Dress in union suit, double socks, flannel, insulated coveralls.

Cover your hands with gloves tucked inside deer hide mittens.

Cover your head with a Farmer Co-op wool cap with earmuffs.

Invest well in footwear. Avoid chilblains.

Heal cracked fingers and toes with teat balm.

Remember how old Bill Belk would take the battery from the Buick
into the house, leave it by the woodstove,
take it back out Sunday mornings
to drive to church.

Stay home. Play cards. Play checkers.

Ignore a February thaw. Spring is months away.

Think of how you hate summer – the
humidity, sweat, and swarming flies.

Heat soup.

Drink black coffee boosted by brandy.

Practice patience.

To Fathers and Sons

The day has only begun, but as your father
I can tell
you are not well.

You stare into your black coffee
and say you barely slept,
your bed a bed of thorns.

It is a golden October day
filled with the light Steinbeck claimed
belongs only to Wisconsin in autumn.

Let's pull on our boots
and take a walk, I suggest. There are
so many trails leading from this place.

At the ridgetop, amongst the falling leaves,
we pause. The view extends miles
but you tell me you've lost your way.

I understand. I was young once, too.
I go on, trying to make things right,
promising you will find your own happiness.

You ask if I talked to my father
about such things and I tell you I did,
a long time ago when I had hair like yours.

And there it is – a smile, a laugh, as you look
at my hairline and joke it must have been
a very, very long time ago.

We go on, father and son, side by side,
through a day suddenly lighter, down a trail
taking us both back home.

To Gary Snyder's, "Sixth-Month Song in the Foothills"

I am fifty years from a used bookstore in Madison, Wisconsin
where I first read your book of poems, *The Back Country.*

I felt my world shift like one does when the trail breaks clear
and suddenly there are peaks, valleys, far-off vistas never seen before.

I went with you into the cold shed to stand
beneath the nests of swallows.
Spring was nearing. There were tools in need of sharpening and repair.

My old life was somewhere far from where I stood. Snow was melting.
I held in my hands the sharpened axe
as I watched the horses nibble brown grass.

Even today, after half a century, I keep a shed
lined with tools. I watch spring
emerge from a Wisconsin winter as I sing a sixth-month song
to the fields beyond.

I have traveled a long way in the direction you pointed – toward
farming, tools, books read by firelight. I am old now but still
upright in the cold shed, sharpening tools, stacking words.

The Lies
I Tell Myself

The Lies I Tell Myself

I held my mother's hand
while she passed away.

I held my father's hand
while he passed away.

I asked all the best questions
and took the answers to heart.

All those hours drunk in bars
were well spent.

Books I never read
would be of little interest.

Someday I'll hike over glaciers
in the north country.

Someday I'll build something,
a fence or shed. Something.

I'll know all the constellations
and teach them to my grandchildren.

There will be no wasted hours,
lost loves, broken friendships.

Many will read my words
and be better off having read them.

Many will read my words.

Simple Wants

I am a man of simple wants.

I want to look across the table
each evening to this woman I love.

I want there to be candles, wine, food.

I want to know
those close to us are well,
what the grandchildren did today.

I want to climb the stairs
on strong legs
and sleep close together.

I know sometimes I want too much.

I want this not to be one of those times.

Along the Wisconsin River

Born landlocked, grounded
in a sea of grass on the Illinois prairie,
I never learned to swim, fish, canoe.

I thought of water as rain.

Still, I came upon this river
in books read
on Midwestern nights too hot for sleep.

Now, far from the prairie
and long past boyhood,
I've found it again
north of the bridge at Prairie du Sac.

Here, the river straightens out
like a paroled felon,
cuts south toward Spring Green.

Evening light upon the water
holds an allure
equal to that of a beautiful woman.

Too late – I am what I am – a landlubber
in long pants and heavy boots.

I wouldn't step a toe in the Wisconsin
if August Derleth himself held my arm.

There are those who have
and they have yet to be found.

Late on Thanksgiving Night in the Nursing Home

The residents have returned
to their rooms.

The skeleton staff
clears the dining tables.

An aide wheels an empty wheelchair
into the vacant lobby.

One lone man remains seated,
savoring his turkey and gravy.

There is single glass of red wine
before him on the table.

Silently, slowly, he raises a toast
to the empty chair across.

Never

what brought us here
must still be here
somewhere
simply misplaced
not lost
dropped somewhere
in the tall
tangled grass
unkept and neglected
over time
left behind
in our hurry
to get to a place
we thought
we needed to be
certain
we of all people
could never lose hold
of something
so precious
it made up
everything we were
everything we loved
so come with me
crawl with me
across the dry dirt
rake with our fingers
tear skin from our knees
never cease
never stand
until we hold
all we never
should have lost

In the Cold

When night
hits twenty below
the Winter House cracks like a rifle shot.

Dreams bolt like startled deer.

Old regrets, new fears
creep close, settle beside me
like a familiar lover.

I linger long awake
under the white winter stars.

Sleep is somewhere
out there
stomping through the woods.

Weekend News

They always lead with war.

Full color missiles, mortars, drone blasts.

The collapse of a sovereign state
on the far side of the globe
brought home
with the touch of the remote.

Complete with fleeing refugees
carrying all they own
in their arms.

Quick shots of the maimed
and the dead
left lying in the streets.

After the commercial,
they pivot
to the car show underway
in the downtown Civic Center.

All the latest models on display.

Bring the family.
Fill up on corn dogs, popcorn, soda.

The cars dazzle
under neon lights and the whole place
has that new car smell.

Duck's Misery

West of the Illinois Central right-of-way, south of Scioto Mills, east
of the Pecatonica River, well north of any ground fit for farming,
Duck's Misery formed into a bed of switchgrass, cattails, milkweed,
and tamarack trees. It was there Glen Kraft pulled up carp and catfish
from the muddy bottoms, carried them home in a tin pail for frying.
It was there Glen Kraft stalked snapper turtles big enough for turtle
stew and snared muskrats in spring loaded traps.

Glen Kraft farmed the old Kraft farm carved out of oak and elm and
brush where he grew up one of eleven kids, the only one that stayed
to home. There was a wooden dairy barn that never saw a swipe of
paint, a corn crib clinging to a fieldstone foundation, and a two-story
farmhouse hidden by black window screens and Creeping Jenny.
Dogs slept under the porch boards, cats in the south windows, and
chickens of all colors pecked through the stoned farmyard.

Glen Kraft worked old Farmall tractors started up by popping the
clutch on a downhill roll. He ground corn and oats with a Farmhand
grinder-mixer and hired out to the neighbors, rattling up and down
the gravel roads covered in grain dust. Folks looked up from their
gardens and the open doorways of cow barns, waved as he passed,
yelled *There goes Glen Kraft*. He wore grey coveralls and a yellow seed
corn cap with ear flaps that flapped in the wind.

It was in the fall of his 57th year, back when the wife was still alive and
to home, Glen Kraft pushed a pile of wet corn into the grinder and
off came four fingers. Betty hauled him to the hospital in Monroe, his
hand wrapped in a feed sack, blood pooling on the floorboards. He
argued with the doctors, stormed out, was back feeding and bedding
stock by nightfall, a plastic bag covering the clean white wrappings.

Word reached Glen Kraft the Olson boys over on the highway were
dealing on a Gehl grinder-mixer – a cheap imitation prone to bad
bearings and twisted auger shafts. Glen Kraft drove in uninvited on a
Farmall M with his Farmhand grinder-mixer bouncing behind. He set
to grind two tons of cob corn in 25 minutes, proving his point. The

Olson farm ran Farmhand from that day on while the Gehl dealer cussed Glen Kraft under his breath.

By her mid-sixties, Betty began talking in circles, forgetting the lit stove, setting her purse in the icebox and the butter in the hall. One day she got lost on her way to the mailbox, wandered off afoot on the township road where she'd lived five decades. The sheriff came across her south of Myers Brother's Lumber and Feed, talking nonsense in the summer heat. She lived two years in the county home before making Glen Kraft a widower.

Then it was all to a little farming between the fences, the barbed wire and woven wire going slack between the bent posts. He took day hikes into Duck's Misery with a fishhook, line, and traps. He fed a hog and steer for the freezer, topped off with venison shot from a blind in the woods Thanksgiving week, the year's first snow covering his shoulders.

He pounded pole spikes into the wooden walls of the barn and sheds, hung up things most folks threw away – old scythes, corn knives, the busted race of a bearing, chains of all gauges and length, drive belts worn smooth by the spinning, odd fits of metal, wood, and rubber. He had a place for everything and everything was in its place.

Wednesday nights, in all weathers, Glen Kraft steered a rusted Ford stock truck down to Johnny Henke's Blue Room Saloon to sit by the potbelly stove or on the front porch, drinking Old Milwaukee beer, talking crops, catfish, and critters. He drove home under the summer stars or the winter stars, light-headed, done socializing for the week.

He'd been gone a spell when people began to wonder. A Wednesday night came and went with Johnny waiting, peering down the road toward the Kraft farm.

Two kids on a hike came upon him in the late light of a December evening along the backside of Duck's Misery, Glen Kraft's body leant down into the thickening ice, his hand ahold of a muskrat trap, all the farming, trapping, fishing, all the making do with one good hand fading from eyes gone blind as the water, staring north by northwest over the old fields.

Listen

You can't have easy digging
all the time.

You can't just sit in the soft seat,
pulling levers,
chomping on a thick cigar.

Some days, you must jump down
into the ditch, shovel
and pickaxe in hand,

start breaking through the rock,
an inch at a time.

Heat

It was Missouri in July
and the heat grew with the corn
grown thick with Johnson grass.

It was six hours of hot hoeing
paid for with cold bottles of Stag
he brought back from town.

It was Four Roses bourbon poured
into a silver shot glass
disguised as a pocket watch.

It was the most goddamn thing
anyone ever saw
he said with a laugh.

It was, we agreed, still
too green to have seen
much of anything at all.

Where There's Smoke

On the way back
from walking the dog

long before the Winter House
comes into view

I smell smoke

the dog bolts ahead
on a dead run

through the window
I see you

standing at the woodstove
stirring supper

I know
our meal is almost ready

I know
you've opened the wine

suddenly I find myself
running as well

CAT Scan

I shiver
bare bottom
on the cold steel table.

Don't move, she says.

Hovering. Adjusting.

So, what's going on?

Can't pee.

That sucks,
she whispers under her breath.

Finally, she leans over.
Her scrubs brush my face.

She presses a red button
and sends me into the machine.

The Educated

The lawn mower belt
flies off,
lands ten feet away in tall grass.

My sons gather around, studying,
offering suggestions.

I add it up in my mind – between us
nearly a half century of higher education.

Advanced degrees in literature, medicine,
law, from the nation's best schools.

Letters behind our names. Titles on doors.

We bump our heads together, lean in
and try to figure out the path of the pulleys.

But we give up.

It proves to be
too much
and not one of us has a clue.

Chance

A blind hog finds an acorn
    every once in a while.

So, I keep my nose to the ground,

sorting through the grass,
poking the leaves,

searching.

Absence

Distance swells
whenever you are away.

As if an ocean suddenly
sprung up between us.

Time slows and I find myself
pacing away the hours.

The dogs grow quiet, their heads
turned toward the door.

I can't help but think
this is life had we never met.

I can't help but think
this is life should you never return.

Your Hair, Before the Snow

Hiking the back trail
through Walking Iron Park
the footing good after a recent thaw
you make your way ahead
and I linger
admiring how your hair
matches
the color of the oak leaves,
the only leaves
in January,
and you turn and say you heard
snow is likely
the sky has that look
almost pewter in color
I point west to clouds
low over the Wisconsin River
you say you love a day like today
and move on beneath the trees
your hair crossed by the wind
the oak leaves lifting
as if they know
the care you've taken to comb
and color
what falls now from beneath your hat
onto your shoulders
drawing me closer
pulling me deeper
into the woods

A Fire

Split elm, oak, black walnut
Broken boards from the pasture fence
Old pages from *The Stephenson Farmer*

A handful of cedar shavings

Strike a wooden match

It takes a while
For the black iron stove to warm
But warm it will

In the meantime
Drink wine

Practice patience

Read poems
Write one

Alone at night
In a Winter House

The Losses

I keep a wary eye on the scorekeeper
Who keeps keeping score, scoring

The losses that beat the wins by a mile
The few wins I manage to chalk up

Over opponents who bob and weave
Managing to flaunt all the rules

I've been too long in the game
I've lost my edge, my pacing, my moves

The big clock on the wall is ticking down
The referee watches and wets his whistle

I know better than to play for overtime
I'll launch a desperation shot at the buzzer

Moving Wild Cattle

They tend to go
in any direction but the one
you want.

A bit like marbles
dropped on the floor.

It helps, my father says,
to be smarter than they are.

Only he has the patience
to light a cigarette
and wait.

Why chase? They can run
as fast as we can.

But I have places to be
and things to do.

Finally, after an hour burned
in the hot summer sun

they're all right there,
right where we want them.

Winter, 1981

You think this is cold?

You think this is snow?

Hell, this is nothing.

Why, back in '81, the lane
blew shut
drifts higher than your head
froze hard as concrete.

Had to drive the old Farmall
back and forth
across the open fields
to the milking barn.

Came in with my face froze
to my hat.

Had to soak in warm water
just to feel my fingers.

That's the way it was
and not a damn thing you could
do about it, either.

If you'd been there
you wouldn't think this global warming
such a bad thing.

Cabin Life

Never much of a mansion man
this cabin suits me fine.

Short on square footage, lacking storage,
I keep only what's essential.

Favorite books. Wooden boxes. Pottery.
A few old tools from the farm in Illinois.

On summer nights there's the deck and stars.
On winter nights a chair close to the fire.

I know one day they'll carry me out feet first.
They'll back up a truck and toss in a life.

I'll make it easy on them. I'll accumulate little.
When the fire goes out, I'll already be ash.

The Voice of Experience

We worked side-by side in the darkening barn,
desperate to beat the rain,
stacking clear up to the rafters,
the last of the haying.

I was fresh out the gate,
throttle pulled wide open.

He was sixty years a bachelor,
laboring for room and board
on farms he'd never own.

Between bales, he leaned close,
asked if I still had that girlfriend he'd seen
come around.

Good, he went on. Now don't be a fool
and do something stupid.

I see that look.

Watch yourself.

Or sure as hell
you'll end up just like me.

The Burning

The heart of the cabin
is the fire
caged in black cast iron
burning, burning.

The heart of my life
is this woman
offering herself to me
burning, burning.

Ruins

The house down the road
where Pickle lived
is busy collapsing
onto itself
broken windows gapped
wide open
a new gap in the shingles
open to rain and sky
outback a pile of beer
and whiskey bottles
an arm's throw from the porch
Pickle's good aim
across the unmown lawn
into the weeds
with a clatter
that broke
the silence of a solo life
one pitch at a time
into the black night
until what little
held in place
broke down
tore up
gave out

My World

There is this thing called the day
standing right in front of me.

It is not yet light.
Dawn is just a thin promise
above the hills in the east.

All the hours are lined up
like dominos
waiting to be knocked down.

I make black coffee.
I check the news and weather.

I think of people I love
waking up in far-away cities.

They'll soon begin their day,
driving straight into traffic,
rushing into tall buildings.

Perhaps a bit under the weather,
distracted, worn down by the grind,
but clocking in, meeting deadlines.

I should be there beside them,
putting my shoulder to the wheel,
pulling something certain from the doubt.

Not refilling my cup,
watching from a window, wondering
what in this world I will do all day.

Nights on the Farm

We laid a pallet of blankets
on the bedroom floor
beside our bed,

close but apart
from the constant twitching
of my body

like an engine overheated
running on
from the day's work.

The only way you could sleep.

In the morning, long
before light, I'd already
be gone,

the tangled blankets
left behind,
tossed upon the floorboards.

Hours later, over breakfast,
the morning milking done,
the whole day ahead,

you would smile
over your coffee, and ask
how I slept.

After Church Stew

The priest drones on
and on
and on.

You look around at girls
in short
Sunday dresses.

You dream ahead
to a swim
or shooting baskets in the yard.

But first, after church,
they serve
After Church Stew.

You push it around
your plate
sorting meat from potatoes.

You chew and chew
but find it all
so very hard to swallow.

Two Barns

A black and white photo
of a barn

stands in the window

where I stand
staring out at the barn.

A Tour of the House I Grew Up In

Come in the back door – only company
used the front.

Hang your hat and coat
on the wall rack in the mud room.
Kick off your boots.

Push down the Pennsylvania Dutch
black iron door latch, step into
the big farmhouse kitchen.

Look up at the exposed beams.

Look around to the printed wallpaper
brought home
from a weekend in Milwaukee.

Admire the pull-out butcher block table,
built by hand
by canning factory carpenters,
not long after the war.

Go on into the dining room.
Spend some time
seated at the formal table,
beneath the chandelier.

Rise and stand before the mirror
of the antique buffet,
holding blue and white place settings,
sterling candlesticks, white linens.

Follow the hallway past the newel post
to the living room of white plaster walls
and gleaming grey woodwork.

Built-in bookcases
extend outward from the fireplace,
filled with the works
of Frost, Michener, Hemingway.

The arranged shelves,
evenly spaced, adorned
with artwork, pottery, framed family photos.

Settle into a Queen Anne chair,
pulled close to the fire.

Go back years, relive
Christmas Eve, Christmas morning,
winter evenings when the lane drifted shut,
when the world seemed a world away.

Then climb the stairwell. Go up
to the second-floor landing.

Wander bedroom to bedroom,
the master with a view
of the barn, visible,
in case of fire or storm.

Trace the age and height
of eight children notched into the woodwork
around a closet door.

Walk the pine floors, sanded smooth,
stained, smooth beneath your feet.

Gaze out from big windows with framed glass
distorted by age and weather.

Look out over the trees and pond,
over the fields of the farm.

Keep climbing – there's a third floor –
pine tongue and groove siding, again
the exposed beams,
one small window you treasured
for a breeze
all those hot, summer nights.

Open the corner cedar closet
where Baba's storm coat hung
for decades,
long and heavy, deep pockets
and fur collar, suited for bad weather.

Sit a while. Listen.

Let this old house
hold you in its arms.

Let what was, be again,
if only for a moment.

Then rise. Retrace your steps,
down stairways, along the hall,
out through the kitchen.

Pull on your boots, hat, coat.

Latch the door
behind you,

and go back into today.

Tracks

Five days gone
doing other things – now
I'm back on the trail.

This familiar ridge in Morton Forest –
old burr oaks, limestone outcroppings,
hard frozen snow.

I come across tracks – my tracks –

See the slightly askew turn of my left foot.
The old familiar pattern of my snow cleats.

Suddenly, I feel I am home, back
doing what I was doing –

before something distant and vague
pulled me away.

Antiques

We were kids
boy
and girl
a car
the whole day
ahead
all around us
open fields
I took a photo
of you
kneeling
by the edge of a creek
gathering leaves
I still have it
here
somewhere
later
we drove over a bridge
to an antique store
filled with old-fashioned
things
the thought
came to us
there in the adorned
aisles
let's grow old
together
let's live
an old-fashioned life
let's become
something
this beautiful
and precious

Endgame

Let there be a window box
outside a window easily opened

filled with red and white geraniums
the colors of Wisconsin

for Wisconsin is where we met
and where we came back to

after all those years of work
and worry on a far-away farm

to settle in our Winter House
under red oaks and white pines

happily tending a window box
happily tending each other

Acknowledgments

Wisconsin Fellowship of Poets 2023 Calendar: "To What We Wore"
The Midwest Quarterly: "In the Farmhouse"
Grey Sparrow Journal: "Memory of My Mother, Burning Trash"
Allium, A Journal of Poetry, and Prose: "To Words"

Thank you!

To Austin, Ryan and Trang, Levi and Brenna, for love and support. To my siblings, who share my love for the farm. To neighbors and friends, who welcome my words into their worlds. To Dale Clark, master craftsman, builder of the Winter House. To my fellow poets, especially Austin Smith, J.D. Whitney, Dion Kempthorne, and always, Gary Snyder. To the literary editors who have published and supported my work over the years, especially Water's Edge Press. To my wonderful friends at Arcadia Books in Spring Green, Wisconsin.

In Loving Memory

Of Robert and Mary Smith, who taught,
and encouraged, and pointed the way.

Of Sheldon and Florene Miller,
who raised a beautiful daughter,
and welcomed a farmer into their world.

Of my poetic mentors,
Michael Mott, Lucien Stryk, Kent Johnson.